HAROLD KLEMP

HU
THE MOST
BEAUTIFUL PRAYER

HAROLD KLEMP

ECKANKAR
Minneapolis
www.Eckankar.org

ABOUT THIS BOOK: *HU, the Most Beautiful Prayer* is compiled from Harold Klemp's writings. These selections originally appeared in his books published by Eckankar. The accompanying CD contains a recording of the HU song; you can play it for spiritual upliftment, or you can sing along.

Printed in USA

Compiled by Sue Jenkins and John Kulick
Edited by Patrick Carroll, Joan Klemp, and Anthony Moore
Cover illustration: Ron Wennekes
Text photo by Robert Huntley
Cover design by Doug Munson

Library of Congress Cataloging-in-Publication Data
Klemp, Harold.
    HU, the most beautiful prayer / Harold Klemp.
      p. cm.
    ISBN 978-1-57043-283-5 (hardback : alk. paper)
  1. Spiritual life—Eckankar (Organization) 2. Prayer—Eckankar (Organization). I. Title.
    BP605.E3K5585 2008
    299'.93—dc22
                                                    2008013904

♾ This paper meets the requirements of ANSI/NISO Z39.48-1992 (Permanence of Paper).

Contents

FOREWORD

Singing HU has been practiced for thousands of years in one form or another for inner attunement. In the same way a musician can use a tuning fork to find the right pitch, the person singing HU tunes in to a higher spiritual awareness.

In most spiritual traditions, sound plays a part in uplifting the individual. Religions such as Christianity, Judaism, and Buddhism have made use of sound in the form of hymns, chants, and prayers to help open the heart and go beyond intellectual knowledge. Muslims, Sufis, and Hindus chant or sing the holy names of God in their monasteries and temples around the world.

One example is the word *alleluia*, a form of the word *HU* that is sung in many hymns and in the famous chorus from Handel's *Messiah*. *Alleluia* is from two words, *Allah* and *HU*, joined together to form the sound "allahu." Over the centuries, it has become the familiar word *alleluia* or *hallelujah.*

We are involved with the uplifting nature of sound and music every day. Look at the positive feelings inspired by songs with personal meaning for us. Just hearing a familiar melody opens us again to another time and place. And consider that our mother's heartbeat is one of the first sounds we experience in this world; then comes her voice. When she sings a lullaby, it's a carrier for love to her child.

In a similar way, HU is a carrier of love between you and God.

HU can be sung silently at work, home, or anytime you feel a need to tune in to a higher perspective on your life. You might try experimenting with it when you face a challenging situation or want to open yourself to a more loving attitude.

Singing HU each day can lead to a deeper

understanding of yourself and why things happen the way they do in your life. It carefully opens your awareness to new viewpoints and attitudes. Anyone can work with the HU regardless of age, background, or religion.

HU, the most beautiful prayer, is a gift to the world.

1

WHY SING HU?

*H*U, this ancient name for God, is a love song to God. You can sing it. And in singing it or holding it in your mind during times of need, it becomes a prayer. It becomes a prayer of the highest sort.

It becomes a nondirected prayer, which means that we're willing to let the Holy Spirit take care of the affairs in our life according to the divine plan instead of our personal plan.

Generally, the reason we're having problems is because our plan was fulfilled.

HU uplifts and purifies us of the evils that make life too much to bear. It heals our wounds, soothes our brow—sweet but mighty name of God.

In all heaven and earth, no name is mightier than HU. It can lift the grieving heart to a temple of solace. A companion in trouble, it is likewise a friend in times of prosperity. And is it any wonder, for HU is Soul's most precious gift from God.

2

A GIFT TO THE WORLD

*H*U is an ancient name for God. It is also a love song to God. All that we do with the word *HU* is to sing it with reverence. It represents the love of God for Soul, and we are Soul. HU represents the enormous love that the Creator has for Its creation.

Divine love has no conditions—it simply loves. God loves, but not because we deserve it or have earned it. The reason is simply that God is love, therefore God loves. We are Soul, God's creation, and It loves us because that is Its nature.

HU can be sung by anyone, whether Christian, Muslim, or of any other religion. It isn't meant to change your religion. HU will enhance it.

Each religion is a classroom. As a Soul finishes one classroom, It goes to another classroom, to another religion—not necessarily a higher one, but another one. Soul chooses Its classrooms of religion on earth until It has learned everything It wishes to learn there.

Eventually Soul finds Its way to the teachings of ECK and learns the song of HU, which I call the most beautiful prayer. This special name for God has a power unlike any other.

3

THE MOST
BEAUTIFUL PRAYER

$\mathcal{A}$ young woman, "Nora," had lost touch with a friend of hers. They hadn't been in contact for eight years. Then her friend, "Suzy," wrote to her. So Nora wrote back about how her life had changed since they'd last been in touch.

Nora explained that in the meantime she'd come in contact with Eckankar and she had learned this word *HU*, this ancient name for God, this love song to God. She also called it the most beautiful prayer.

Nora didn't hear from her friend again for some time. Then Suzy went into the hospital for treatment for a recurring medical condition. Because of her treatments, she had to get injections for the pain every half hour throughout the night.

Suzy was very frightened of the pain and the shots she needed to endure the pain. She was just terrified of having to go back to the

11

hospital because she'd been through the painful treatments before.

But then she remembered what Nora had told her about HU, the most beautiful prayer. And she thought, *Well, there's no harm. Might as well try it. I've got nothing else facing me except this pain and fear.*

So Suzy began to sing HU. As she sang HU, a sense of peace and calm came over her. And throughout the entire night, she didn't have any pain and didn't need any of the injections.

The next morning, her doctor asked her, "Why didn't you need any injections last night? Why were you able to pass the night in quiet sleep?"

She said, "Because of HU, the most beautiful prayer."

"What do you mean?"

Suzy explained that a friend of hers had told her about this in a letter, and she had the letter with her.

"May I read the letter?" the doctor asked.

The doctor read the letter, and he was very impressed with HU. He could see that it had the power to heal in this woman's life, so he made it part of her physical therapy. Three times a day she was to chant HU—which was quite interesting because Suzy was a Catholic.

Then Suzy had to see two other doctors. These two doctors also asked her about how she had gotten through the night without any pain.

She said, "Because of this HU." And they wanted to know about it too. HU—the most beautiful prayer.

This is just one example of how to help yourself spiritually. There are many areas where HU works.

During the time you're singing HU, you are saying to Divine Spirit, "I've opened myself to you. Give me the understanding and the wisdom to meet the waves of life—the problems, troubles, and whatever else. Give me the strength to meet

13

life." This is basically what we do when we do this spiritual exercise.

But don't expect HU to work as you want, because God's love, as it comes down and heals, does things its way. Not my will, but thine be done—the nondirected prayer.

4
WHEN YOUR DAY IS HARD

The world is going so fast, and the pace is so speeded up. You can call this the pace of karma. It means the interaction of people with people has been speeded up so greatly that we have to find some time to be quiet by ourselves.

This is the only way to make contact with the inner force, Divine Spirit, the Inner Master, or whatever you want to call this power.

There are different methods of quieting the outer senses and seeing what happens within. You can do this no matter what faith you are. You can do it with prayer if you like.

You can, for example, very quietly contemplate on the Lord's Prayer. Or you can visualize a Master who is compatible with you. Someone you respect. You can look to Jesus, to one of the ECK Masters, or to a saint who means something to you.

The purpose of doing this is to establish trust and confidence before you go to that stillness within. Then you begin actively looking for the Light or listening for the Sound of God. There may be a number of different sounds you will hear, which is the Audible Life Stream, the Holy Spirit, vibrating at a certain speed at a certain level. Sometimes it sounds like whistles. It can sound like running water. It can sound like the swishing of a wire whipping through the air, or it can be music.

The Sound will have many different manifestations. What it's doing is cleansing and uplifting you in your consciousness so you can have a broader understanding of the life you lead. And this is for your benefit, of course.

So often we run into problems in our everyday life, and things go wrong. Right away we think, *It's somebody else's fault.* If things go wrong, it's never us. Yet if we would just take a moment to stand back and look things over, we would find they may be going wrong because of the way we are feeling that day.

We may be feeling angry, fearful, frenzied because of deadlines we feel we can't meet, overworked, or anxious. The more anxious and upset we get, the worse our day goes. Suddenly other people are getting on our nerves, and we're getting on other people's nerves. And at the end of the day, we go home exhausted. "I don't know how many more days like that I can stand," we say.

Very few people realize they caused this day themselves. If only they'd remember to stop and sing HU.

A woman I'll call "Rita" and her family went through some extreme difficulties in their community. They're very respected community leaders, working at high levels in the educational field in state government, but in their hometown the bias against them was quite strong.

Rita works in a very responsible position as a school president. When she took the job, she expected people to be ethical. But there were jealousies. Some people were jealous that she, a woman from outside the state, had been named president. Other people who had been at the institution for years thought they had earned the right to have that position instead of her. And they used threats against her property and things of this nature to frighten her and her family, to try to break down her will.

But when she went to work each day and faced these people who were threatening her and lying to her, she kept trusting in the ECK, Divine Spirit, and she sang HU.

She was trying to make the educational institution as ethical and outstanding as it could be. As the months passed, a lot of decay and corruption within the organization came to the surface. But because she sang HU and put her situation into the hands of Divine Spirit, she finally started gaining support. The community has slowly come forward to support her in her work.

HU, this name for God, can be very useful if you can remember to sing it at a time like this.

When your day is hard, remember to sing HU.
It puts you back in line with the Holy Spirit.

5

A NONDIRECTED PRAYER

*H*U is a prayer, but it is a pure prayer which does not direct God to do anything.

Prayer in other groups often goes wrong because people use it to tell God what to do. They say, "God, I don't feel well—please make me better." But maybe God made you sick to teach you something, perhaps about the kind of foods you've been eating.

A person who is very distressed may say, "Please, God, make me feel better." Could it be that you are upset about something that's none of your business? Maybe God is trying to teach you not to be distressed by a matter that doesn't concern you. This happens over and over, but what does it take for a person to learn?

There's a right way to pray and a wrong way to pray. The right way to pray is to sing a song of love to God, whether it's HU or another song.

25

It's the height of human folly and ignorance to design a prayer to tell God what to do, as if God does not know what's happening.

There is nothing wrong with saying, "God, do Thy will." This is fine, because God is going to do Its will anyway.

It is said that God knows even when a sparrow falls but that God doesn't stop the sparrow from falling. This is an important point. The cycles of nature are run by divine will and divine love. The reason we resist them is because we in the human state of consciousness generally cannot see farther than the end of our nose.

The Spiritual Exercises of ECK, like singing HU, are simple contemplations; in a way they are the ECK equivalent to prayer.

In contemplation you shut your eyes, listen, and wait for God to speak to you. It's a whole different approach. Through the spiritual exercises and this contemplative effort, you learn to listen to the Voice of God. The Voice of God is the Holy Spirit, which we call the ECK.

The pure prayer to God is simply a song of love to the Creator. And the best one I know is the song of HU.

Another way that HU sometimes helps people is by healing. A member of Eckankar named Heidi had a very young nephew—four years old—who hadn't seen her too often because they live in different parts of the country. The child had swallowed something and went into a coma. The doctors did everything they could, but the child was in a coma for two days.

At this point, Heidi decided she'd do something. She talked to the Inner Master, the Mahanta. "Inwardly I'm going to invite the parents and the child to sing HU with me in the heavenly worlds if they want to," she said.

So she sat down in contemplation and began to sing HU. She was careful not to make it a directed prayer, like saying, "Please, God, make this child well. Whatever's wrong, make my nephew wake up." It was nothing like that. She just did this spiritual exercise in a nondirected way: Thy will be done, not mine. Or as we say in ECK, May the blessings be.

Shortly after that, the little boy suddenly opened his eyes and saw a nurse. The first thing he said when he saw the nurse was, "Are you Heidi?"

The little boy was awake and well because he and his parents had joined Heidi on the inner planes singing HU.

The little boy remembered the inner experience. The parents didn't, though, because as we get older, we often lose the gift of seeing the messengers or the miracles of God. They get crowded out in the rush of everyday living.

6

RESTING IN THE ARMS OF GOD

"*S*tan," from Ohio, said that at about one o'clock one morning, he became aware of a humming sound. He sat on the edge of the bed and listened to it grow in intensity. He then reclined and totally surrendered to the experience of the moment and was conscious of the sound flowing through him as it extended outward into the space surrounding him. The serenity and peacefulness of the experience stayed with him until he entered into the sleep state.

After the experience, Stan remarked, "If this is what it's like to rest in the arms of God, I welcome it anytime, anyplace, and under any conditions."

No matter which inner sound you hear, it's the sound of the Holy Spirit uplifting you. It's the sound of the Holy Spirit making changes in you which will leave you different tomorrow than what you were yesterday.

And these changes, which begin at the Soul level, at the heart of you, work their way out into the outer world in time. They begin to change your behavior into more ethical behavior. Into higher actions, even though the goal of spiritual unfoldment is not ethics or higher actions.

In the same way, wisdom, power, and freedom are not the goal for the seeker of God. These are attributes which come to one who has God-Realization. In other words, "Seek ye first the kingdom of God . . . and all these things shall be added unto you."

What I'm saying is seek the highest, and the rest of life will fall into place. And this is the role of HU.

Another young man, "Larry," learned a valuable lesson about singing HU as he was driving home one night. He was on a winding fifty-seven-mile stretch of road, with very little traffic.

About halfway home he happened to glance at the gas gauge. Uh-oh—the needle was on empty. He had forgotten to check it before he left home. Now he started to worry. He still had about thirty miles to go on this dark, deserted road. What if he ran out of gas before he got home?

I know what I can do, he thought. *I'll sing HU!*

What was his purpose in singing HU? To give him enough gas to get home, of course. The empty tank was his own oversight, but why go through any inconvenience if he didn't have to?

Over and over he sang HU, trying to maintain high hopes that the ECK would get him out of this fix. If he just kept singing HU, maybe he could make it all the way home.

Suddenly an inner voice broke through, interrupting his thoughts. It said, "Do you want gas or God?"

We often sing HU when we are in trouble, but that should never overshadow its true function. It isn't meant to fill gas tanks, heal broken bones, or get us an A on a test we haven't studied for.

We should never lose sight of the fact that HU is the holy name of God. Its purpose is to draw us closer, in our state of consciousness, to the Divine Being.

"OK, I understand," Larry said out loud. Once he got the point, he was able to totally surrender to the situation he had set in motion, and realize that even if he ran out of gas, the problem was not insurmountable.

The lesson he learned was invaluable; even more so because it came at a time when he was right near the edge, anxious and afraid. We are usually more alert, aware, and alive at that point where we fear for our survival than when we are happy and contented.

He did make it home, by the way.

7

To see your life more clearly

When you sing the name of God with love, the bindings and bands that constrain Soul will begin to unwind. Not all at once but very slowly, at a rate you can understand and accept. As these bindings are released, Soul rises in spiritual freedom.

As Soul, you are like a balloon that rises above the ground. The higher you go, the farther you can see. And the farther you can see, the better you can plan your life.

Here's a simple spiritual exercise you can try. As you sit in contemplation, close your eyes and sing HU a few times, then become quiet.

Listen to the sounds you hear coming in from the physical world. Try to identify each one as it comes to your attention, and then eliminate it. One by one, take each sound—an airplane flying over, a cricket, the hum of the refrigerator—and imagine yourself putting it in a basket.

As you keep taking away the sounds that you can identify, you will discover the Sound that always is. HU, the sound behind all sounds. The Word of God.

This spiritual exercise will help you hear it.

8

*L*OOKING

FOR THE LIGHT

$\mathcal{J}$ust as the spiritual exercise in the previous chapter can help you hear the Sound, this one can help you see the Light of God. You begin this exercise by sitting comfortably and putting your feet flat on the floor. Interlace your fingers with your palms up. Or you can just fold your hands in your lap—whichever feels more comfortable. Close your eyes, and look inwardly at the spot between the eyebrows, the Spiritual Eye. Now look for the Light. Visualize a doorway. Visualize a doorway, and see white light coming through it.

Don't look directly at it, but make believe you're looking at the doorway off to either your left or right. Look in an oblique manner. Think of it this way: If you have been reading in a dark room with a bright light, and then you get up and go into another room, you're blind when you look straight ahead. But if you turn your head to the side, using your peripheral vision, you can see. The same principle applies here.

So put your attention on this doorway at the Spiritual Eye, and look at it from an angle.

Visualize yourself walking to the doorway. Go to the left of it. See if you can see better. Or if you can see better on the right, go to the right.

Then very softly, inwardly to yourself, sing HU. Do it in a long, drawn out breath HU-U-U-U. Or, if you prefer, you can sing "God" or another spiritual name or sound which is special and important to you.

Look at the doorway through which the white light is coming, and in time you should see a blue light or a blue globe or a blue star. This marks the presence of Divine Spirit, or the Mahanta, the Inner Master.

9
SHOW ME LOVE

$\mathscr{O}$ne day the following experience took place while "Emily," a member of Eckankar, and a friend were out walking in nature. As they walked Emily began to tell her friend about all the love she had experienced at an Eckankar seminar.

They came to a clearing and found themselves on top of a cliff that rose out of the forest. A clear lake sparkled below; overhead, the sky was a brilliant blue. *What a perfect day*, Emily thought.

Turning to her friend she said, "In one of the workshops at the seminar, we were told that if we wanted to find divine love, we could sing HU quietly within ourselves. At the same time we could say: 'Show me love, Mahanta. Show me love, Mahanta.' This seems like a perfect time to do it."

And so, standing high atop a cliff overlooking the sparkling blue lake, Emily began to sing HU. "Show me love, Mahanta," she said silently. "Show me love, Mahanta."

All of a sudden a small flock of birds came fluttering down. Some landed on the ground in front of her while others perched in a nearby tree.

The Inner Master nudged her, "Hold out your hand." She felt silly, but she put out her hand. One little bird flew down from the tree and lit on it.

"This can't be," Emily said, laughing with joy. She felt the love of the ECK and the Mahanta coming through the little bird. The love was so strong and pure that she began to weep. She realized the ECK cared so much for her that It would show her Its love even through the humblest of Its creatures.

They left the cliff and continued on their walk. About two hours later, they came back the same way. "I'm going to try it again," she said.

Silently she chanted HU and said, "Show me love, Mahanta. Show me love." She almost couldn't believe it: another flock of birds flew down, she held out her hand, and once again, a little bird landed on it.

Emily knew then that the love of the ECK is real; that the love of the ECK is truth. It is Light and Sound, and It will show Itself through the humblest of Its creatures—if only we will be the humblest of Its creatures.

10
ℒET ME
SOUL TRAVEL

$\mathcal{D}$eborah, from New York, tells of meeting "Bill," a bioengineering professor, and "Liz," his eleven-year-old daughter. Both had sleep disorders. Bill had trouble getting to sleep at night, and when he did sleep, he slept poorly. He was always on edge. Liz was a sleepwalker. Here you've got a dad and daughter, both having problems with sleep.

So Deborah told him about singing HU. And when he got home, he taught his daughter how to sing HU to calm things down for herself.

Now, Bill's belief system had been that when you die, that's the end of it. You're gone like a puff of smoke. Poof! The life you lived here has no more significance than a puff of smoke. And this had always scared him.

He thought, *There's got to be more than this.* But worse, he felt he was passing on this legacy of fear to his daughter and that's why she was sleepwalking.

So they did what Deborah said: "Do the technique of singing HU when you're trying to go to sleep. Just imagine an open door, and walk through it."

It was a good beginning, because now Bill could at least fall asleep. Then in the middle of the night he'd wake up, wide awake as ever. That bothered him, except there was one benefit that hadn't been there before: If something had been puzzling him, he now saw the answer to it. This was something that hadn't happened before. So it was a good beginning, but he still has a ways to go.

His daughter did this HU technique too. As she sang HU and walked through the open door, she began having these wonderful dreams. She slept completely through the night sometimes. The first time this happened, Bill sent an e-mail to Deborah saying, "It works. She's having really good dreams."

Then Liz had a dream where she was snowboarding. She was going down a hill on a board, and she said it was so real. It was more real than things out here, and it was just a lot of fun! Deborah said, "If you'd like to try to repeat the experience tonight, you can do that again, but this time, take my dog with you. Invite my dog to go along."

Next morning, Deborah got another e-mail from Bill. He said, "Liz did just as you said. She invited your dog, and everything in that Soul Travel experience was exactly the same, except your dog was running down the hill with her."

Deborah had explained to Bill that Soul Travel is you living and being aware in full consciousness at a finer level of existence than you already are at. So this was quite an experience for both father and daughter, and the lessons were good too. They learned to play the *HU: A Love Song to God* CD. They said, "Hmm, that's worth it." And now they sing HU every night.

I would like to encourage you to try a spiritual exercise every evening before you go to sleep. One way is to just shut your eyes and sing HU for about five minutes.

And if you wish, you can say to the Mahanta, the Inner Master, "It's OK; take me to the place where I can learn whatever is important for my spiritual unfoldment. Let me Soul Travel. Let me see what it's like. I'd like to try it, and you have my permission."

11
KEY TO A
HAPPIER LIFE

The Light and Sound of God are the two aspects of the Holy Spirit that equal divine love. The highest form of love that you can bring into your life is through the Light and Sound. That's what we look for. And that's why Eckankar is called the Religion of the Light and Sound of God.

These are the two aspects of the Holy Spirit. And the Holy Spirit is the Voice of God.

When a person walks with God, he finds joy in the everyday things he does. Gradually his life begins to expand. The person is becoming godlike.

Try this simple spiritual exercise to help you hear and see the two aspects of God, the Light and Sound.

Go somewhere quiet. Sit or lie down in a comfortable place. Put your attention on your

Spiritual Eye, a point just above and behind your eyebrows. With eyes lightly shut, begin to sing a holy word or phrase, such as HU, God, Holy Spirit, or Show me thy ways, O Lord. But fill your heart with love before you approach the altar of God, because only the pure may come.

Be patient. Do this exercise for several weeks, for a limit of twenty minutes each time. Sit, sing, and wait. God speaks only when you are able to listen.

If you want to lift yourself to a higher state of consciousness—so that the political issues, the family issues, the social issues of the day do not throw you out of balance, so that you can find a happier, more contented life while you're living here—sing HU, the most beautiful prayer.

12

THE AGE-OLD NAME FOR GOD

*H*U is foremost among the ancient names for God. It is the true, universal name drawn from the Sound Current Itself, for HU is woven into the language of life.

It is the sound of all sounds. It is the wind in the leaves, falling rain, thunder of jets, singing of birds, the awful rumble of a tornado. Again, Its sound is heard in laughter, weeping, the din of city traffic, ocean waves, and the quiet rippling of a mountain stream.

HU is both a name for God and a sound of the Audible Life Stream, which we know as the ECK, or Holy Spirit. HU is a charged name for God that can spiritually uplift the people of any religion.

Every religion ever created by ECK (the Holy Spirit) was to breathe new life into the spiritual evolution of the human race. All religions are of

ECK. All, especially in the beginning, provide their followers with a new understanding of life. The development of each religion sees the rise of leaders who reshape and restructure the original teachings to fit the changing times.

Therefore, records left by past religious writers still bear a message for us today. In Christianity, early church fathers grappled with the nature of God, Soul, truth, angels, and heaven.

Was God almighty? If so, what explained the existence of Satan?

How many angels could dance on the head of a pin? Was this question driven by idle curiosity, or were the church fathers searching for an Achilles' heel of Soul? Might angels, good or evil, be of such fine substance as to penetrate the shell of Soul? If Soul's defenses were so exposed to an outside influence, even that of an angel, did this restrict one's free will? Could this alter Soul's salvation?

Questions like these have churned the dust

since mankind's arrival on earth. In each succeeding age, humanity has developed a rash of ideas about what God is and what God is not. Yet, all remains in the realm of opinion.

Not a single church father from orthodox religion has been able to tell his people: "This is what God is!" and be right about it. He *believes* he knows the true spiritual relationship that exists between God and the individual, but his is also only an untried opinion.

In this lies the strength of Eckankar. It also comes to people with a message about the divine mysteries. Yet how it passes along this knowledge is beyond anything ever found.

Its ultimate authority rests not with a personality. Its authority is HU, the universal name for God.

This word has a spiritual force that speaks volumes by itself. It has little need for a human agent, except for the Light Giver. He is the Mahanta, the Living ECK Master, who links Soul with the Sound Current. He helps each find spiritual freedom by passing along this forgotten, holy name for God.

The word is HU. It depends upon no human authority for validation. No priest, minister, or spiritual figure can say HU is this or that. It is what it is. From a practical standpoint, it is love's golden thread, drawing Soul closer to God, like an infant to its parent.

Anytime you sing HU as a love offering to God, the Lord of all creation, your heart fills with the Light and Sound of God. They are the twin aspects of ECK, the Holy Spirit.

HU, the name of God, brings us into a holy alliance with the Light and Sound, the Word of God. Should the worlds tremble and all else fail, HU carries us into the ocean of God's love and mercy.

So sing HU softly, gently. Once among the most secret names of God, the Order of Vairagi

Adepts* has now brought it into the world for the upliftment of all. It is for those who desire true love, true freedom, wisdom, and truth.

In time, people everywhere will have the chance to sing this age-old, universal name for God. This is a new cycle in the spiritual history of the human community.

It will all be due to HU, the most beautiful prayer.

---

*The Vairagi Adepts, or ECK Masters, are spiritual guides people have looked to since the beginning of time for guidance, protection, and divine love.

About the Author

Author Harold Klemp is known as a pioneer of today's focus on "everyday spirituality." He was raised on a Wisconsin farm and attended divinity school. He also served in the U.S. Air Force.

In 1981, after years of training, he became the spiritual leader of Eckankar, Religion of the Light and Sound of God. His mission is to help people find their way back to God in this life.

Harold Klemp speaks each year to thousands of seekers at Eckankar seminars. Author of more than sixty books, he continues to write, including many articles and spiritual-study discourses. Harold Klemp's inspiring and practical approach to spirituality helps thousands of people worldwide find greater freedom, wisdom, and love in their lives.